Old NORTH BERWICK

by
Bruce Jamieson

Melbourne Road, North Berwick.

© Bruce Jamieson 2000
First published in the United Kingdom, 2000,
by Stenlake Publishing
Telephone / Fax: 01290 551122

ISBN 1 84033 107 0

THE PUBLISHERS REGRET THAT THEY CANNOT SUPPLY
COPIES OF ANY PICTURES FEATURED IN THIS BOOK.

ACKNOWLEDGEMENTS

The publishers would like to thank Robert Grieves for providing the
pictures that appear on the front cover, inside front cover and page 31.

The former St Mary's Rest Home in Old Abbey Road is now part of the
properties called 'Elwyn' and 'Matruh'.

INTRODUCTION

It is unclear when North Berwick first became inhabited. The remains of early man are sparse: a shell midden at Castle Hill; some neolithic evidence on the West Links; an Iron Age cattle compound on the slopes of Berwick Law. It is also uncertain whether North Berwick rose to prominence through its harbour or its religious connections. What is known is that a pilgrims' ferry, taking travellers over to Fife, began in the thirteenth century and a hospice was constructed to cater for the visitors, probably in the vicinity of the town's rudimentary harbour. The travellers' hospice may have been connected to a Cistercian abbey, consecrated by Bishop David de Bernham in 1242. In 1371, the lands of North Berwick, which had been in the possession of the Earls of Fife, passed to William, first Earl of Douglas. It may be him sitting on the ferry boat which is still depicted on the town's crest: the heraldic coat of arms properly described as 'a lymphad [a Scottish galley] with sails furled, flying a pennon of the flag of Scotland, rowed by 4 mariners in Kilmarnock bonnets.'

The Douglases made their headquarters in the massively fortified Castle of Tantallon and held sway over the town of North Berwick, whose fortunes grew as the number of pilgrims rose to some 10,000 a year: quite a colossal influx into a township of 700 souls. The prosperity of North Berwick saw it pass through the hands of the Lauders, the Homes, the Dicks of Braid and the (Hamilton) Dalrymples.

North Berwick probably became a royal burgh through a charter of King Robert II in 1373 which gave the community the rights to hold a market and charge customs dues at its harbour. The small medieval port grew into an important trading harbour and the town's fishing industry thrived. However, the sixteenth century saw a decline in North Berwick's fortunes. A raid by the English in 1544 almost totally destroyed the town. Pilgrimages dropped away following the Reformation and consequently North Berwick's standing declined. The first Protestant minister was John Young who still led the townsfolk's worship in the pre-Reformation kirk at the harbour. In 1590, this became the scene of one of Scotland's most famous witchcraft trials following a meeting there, apparently between the Devil and 200 witches. The sixteenth century also saw the last prioress of the town's nunnery, Margaret Home, being forced to give up religious lands and rich endowments to members of the local landed gentry.

In the seventeenth century, several curious visitors travelled to visit the town and the famous Bass Rock, including King James VI, Dr William Harvey (discoverer of the circulation of blood) and Oliver Cromwell, whose troops demolished the fortifications of Tantallon. The Auld Kirk also collapsed, its foundations eaten away by the depredations of the sea, and the town's congregation moved into a new church in Kirk Ports. For almost 200 years, nothing much changed in the sleepy, seaside backwater. The Jacobite rebellion passed it by: the only local incident being a siege of the Bass Rock which had been held by a small band of pro-Stewart stalwarts. Fishing and farming remained the mainstays of the area. The harbour was improved and grain warehouses built.

It was hoped that the coming of the railway in 1850 would lead to a rapid growth in the town's status. This was not the case in the areas of trade and industry, but instead in the increasingly popular pastime of salt water bathing. North Berwick became a Victorian and Edwardian spa town of worldwide fame, and thousands flocked to sample its health-giving waters and clear sea-air. The harbour became a venue for pleasure trips as well as fishing and trading ventures, and in 1872 the first harbour master was appointed at a salary of £5 per year. One of the most famous harbour masters was Daddy Marr, who was still in post in 1930, aged 95. In that year he was given an assistant whom he outlived!

In the late nineteenth and early twentieth centuries, thousands flocked into the town to swim in the sea or in the new, open-air swimming pool. They watched the pierrots on the esplanade, entered sand modelling competitions on the east or west beach (one competition in 1905 attracted 185 entrants!), sailed model boats on the yachting pond or played golf on the world-famous links. It was recorded that on one day in 1903, playing on the same golf course were: the Prime Minister; the Speaker of the House of Commons; four MPs; two bishops; three eminent professors; Field Marshall, Lord Kitchener; two generals and a famous Tibetan explorer. Regular visitors to the town included Prime Minister Asquith; A. J. Balfour MP, R. H. Haldane, Secretary for War, and lords and ladies galore.

The final seal of approval was given by a visit to the burgh by King Edward VII, when a sumptuous dinner was held in his honour at The Knoll. To accommodate the growing influx of visitors, several hotels sprang up including Bradburys, Warrenders, the Tantallon; the Redcroft; the Royal and the Marine.

Meanwhile, life on the sea went on with its share of successes and tragedies. A permanent lifeboat was stationed in the town and a special launching slipway built in 1871. Although the craft were designed to save lives (and indeed they did on many occasions), the lifeboats also played a part in the social life of the elegant watering hole and Lifeboat Day was a grand, ceremonial occasion.

The First World War had a dramatic effect on the fishing life of the town. Not until 1918, when the German fleet surrendered in the Forth, did events return to some normality. But things had changed. The pleasure boats which had plied to and from Galloway's Pier never returned. High society increasingly took their vacations abroad. Several hotels, such as Seabank and the Tantallon never recovered from being used as soldiers' billets during the war years. For a time the Tantallon Hotel became a St Dunstan recuperation home for war blinded.

The burgh tried valiantly to recreate its old elegance and a succession of enlightened town councils led by far-sighted provosts did their best. New tennis courts and putting greens were created. The pool was given several facelifts, new chutes and state-of-the-art diving boards. The galas continued, to be joined by floodlit swimming evenings after the installation of electric lighting in the 1930s. A Harbour Pavilion was built to host concerts and dances.

Considerable land was bought at this time by the town council from the lord of the manor, Sir Hew Hamilton Dalrymple, including the Law; the Glen with its Ladies' Walk and the old Mills of Kinteath; and large areas for house building. The town's population began to increase – especially after the construction of council housing in the Lochbridge, Glenburn and Craigleith areas. Sir Hew Hamilton Dalrymple also sold Tantallon Castle to the Board of Works in the 1920s and an extensive renovation programme was undertaken to conserve its ancient fabric.

The Second World War again disrupted life in North Berwick, with the movement of vessels in the Forth restricted. The Harbour Pavilion was used as a soldiers' barracks and a NAAFI canteen. Other local buildings were pressed into military service including the Tantallon Hotel and several stately homes. Even the magnificent Marine Hotel, once the residence of princes, earls and rich Americans, became a secret development base for the REME.

A branch of the Home Guard, with its HQ in the Hope Rooms, was set up under the command of Lt. Colonel Douglas Blake of Norham in Marmion Road: their two pound anti-tank gun was hidden in the caddies' shelter on the West Links. An ARP unit was set up in the Hamilton Dalrymple townhouse, The Lodge. Trenches were dug on golf courses; anti landing-craft barricades sprung up; anti-tank blocks were erected and mines strewn along the coast from North Berwick through the neighbouring villages of Dirleton, Gullane and Aberlady. An observation post was set up on the ancient Castle Hill and the coastguards manned a special watch on Platcock Rocks. Perhaps the most exciting events were the crash-landing of a German Heinkel near Lime Grove, and the rescuing of a crashed British bomber crew by the Pearson family in their fishing boat off Craigleith Island.

Once again, North Berwick recovered to be a noted seaside resort, but the 1950s and sixties saw its traditional attractions challenged by growing competition from overseas holidays and a more sophisticated population. However, the town survived and was a wonderful place to be brought up in. Indeed, it is still one of the loveliest seaside resorts in the country, despite the fact that much has changed, including the closure of the outdoor pool and the replacement of the Harbour Pavilion with a Seabird Observation Centre.

These views, many of which have never been published before, reveal the changes which have affected Old North Berwick and its neighbouring villages. My thanks go to Alistair and Irene Stewart for their invaluable research assistance.

Bruce Jamieson, 2000.

Driving across the flat farmlands of East Lothian, there is no mistaking the whereabouts of North Berwick. The conical, volcanic mass of Berwick Law rears 613 feet above the town and marks it out from many miles around. From the twelfth to the sixteenth century, the Law belonged to a Cistercian nunnery whose prioress was responsible for lighting the warning beacon on the summit. Such a bonfire blazed in 1544 to warn of an invading English army under the Earl of Hertford. In 1803 a signal station was permanently manned during the Napoleonic War, under the command of Lt. Leyden RN and three naval ratings. If the French fleet was sighted, military HQ in Edinburgh was to be alerted by the lighting of a bale-fire. The small Law stone bothy in which the garrison was billeted was partly dismantled in 1815, although its ruins still remain, along with more recent constructions from World War II. In recent times the summit of the Law has seen many great fires lit to commemorate such events as the coronations of monarchs and the victory celebrations after two world wars. A whale's jawbone was originally erected in 1709. When it blew down in 1933 a replacement was put up along with a flagstaff from the ship *Chancellor*.

5

WEST END, NORTH BERWICK.

The view from the Law across the Firth of Forth and down on to the royal burgh of North Berwick is quite spectacular. The name of the town probably derives from the Old English for 'barley town' (the North being added to distinguish it from Berwick on Tweed). By the time this view was posted (in 1939), the town had grown inland from its coastal origins and had linked up with North Berwick Mains Farm. This was originally an early eighteenth century farm steading but, as can be seen in the foreground, had been developed into a substantial agricultural enterprise with a fine, early nineteenth century farmhouse built of red Law stone.

North Berwick originated by the sea and, for centuries, the population made their living from it. Although it was its fine beaches and associated seaside attractions which brought it subsequent fame, it was as a pilgrim base for travellers, making their way across the Firth of Forth to Fife, that the town first rose to prominence. At its height, some 10,000 pilgrims a year made the journey by sea over to Earlsferry on their way to visit the relics of Scotland's patron saint at the shrine in St Andrews. Many would stay in hospices and religious establishments in and around the town. To this day, the town crest carries a depiction of an early ferry boat being rowed across the nine mile passage. At the stern sits William, first Earl of Douglas, who acquired both North Berwick and Earlsferry from the Earls of Fife in 1371.

THE HARBOUR, NORTH BERWICK

The sea continued to be the focal point of North Berwick life. The old harbour was deepened in 1804 and a boom was installed across the entrance to protect shipping from rough seas. The number of fishing boats operating from the port increased from just two in 1692 to nine in 1840 and thirty in 1881. In 1827 the North Berwick Fishing Company was formed to regulate business, and the herring trade did particularly well. In 1859 a roup of herring stances on the quayside raised the sum of £175 and hundreds of seaweed-lined barrels of fish were sent off annually to the Billingsgate fish market in London.

Most of the goods entering and leaving the town arrived and departed by sea: coal from Bo'ness and Fife; cattle feed and fertilisers from England; potatoes and grain being despatched to markets in Britain and overseas. After the further deepening of the harbour in 1831, vessels of up to 50 tons could enter the basin. Two Law stone warehouses were constructed in 1806 and 1807 to accommodate the growing grain trade. Ownership of these stores passed through various hands before settling down into the possession of James Hope of Fenton Barns and John Brodie of Scougall. A kiln for drying grain was built to the east. The properties eventually fell into the possession of the Hislop family until the town council acquired them in the 1930s. The western granary became a fishing store while the remainder was used as room and kitchen housing before being converted to flats in 1970 by architect Mary Tindall.

Life at the harbour centred around the fishing community whose lifestyle and living conditions have been beautifully captured in the late Ben Millar's *Tales of Old North Berwick*. Many lived in Harbour Terrace and Heriot Row (to the right of this 1920s Valentine's view) named after the builder, John Heriot, who constructed the houses in the 1860s and seventies. Fifteen houses, accommodating some 60 residents, were served by just five toilets and six water taps. Access to the western accommodation was by means of the winding 'Jubilee Stair' constructed in 1887. The 'Wee Stairs' and 'Big Stairs' served the rest of the rabbit-warren of landings and corridors and many a stair-heid argument was waged on each of the three floors. Life was basic and often hard: a far cry from the lifestyles of the yachting fraternity who increasingly used the harbour for pleasurable pursuits.

Pleasure Boat returning to Harbour, North Berwick. 31.

East Lothian Yacht Club was founded in 1900 and soon afterwards moved into the building in the centre of this 1950s view. Next door is the Fishermen's Hall, built in 1883. The pleasure boat in the foreground is the *St Baldred* which replaced an earlier launch of the same name in 1927. Other pleasure craft included the *St Nicholas* and the *Britannia*. To the left is the brick-arched 'Sun Parlour' constructed in 1939 to provide shelter for visitors to the town on inclement summer days.

Pleasure craft had been sailing in and around North Berwick for many years. The first, the *William Scott*, the *Integrity* and the *May*, were operated by the firm of Steedman, Hanson and Dykes. Next on the scene was Jamieson's *Fiery Cross*, after which came the Galloway Saloon Steam Packet Company. They constructed a pier off the Platcock Rocks in 1887 and began cruises on the *Stirling Castle* and the ship pictured here, the *Tantallon Castle*. She was a 210-foot craft, designed to carry 800 passengers and purchased in 1899 for £15,686. A guidebook of the time describes her has having 'a main saloon, sumptuously panelled in oak with Greek pilasters in walnut and gold and couches upholstered in gold Utrecht velvet'.

This boat, awaiting a long line of passengers queuing along Galloway's Pier, is the *Redgauntlet*. The postcard dates from 1912 – the year when the ship had its best season, bringing thousands of trippers from Leith, Portobello, Elie and Leven to North Berwick. All pleasure cruising stopped at the outbreak of war in 1914, and although the pier was put up for sale in 1919, there were no takers. By 1926 it was in a state of considerable disrepair and by 1936 it was estimated that at least £40,000 was required to make it safe for public use. The lower level was and still is used at low tide by small launches taking visitors on trips around the islands of Bass Rock and Fidra, but the pier has never regained its past glory.

North Berwick grew in popularity as a seaside resort when the health-giving properties of salt water bathing were advertised in the Victorian era. In the Edwardian period, the burgh merited the title of the Biarritz of the North and thousands of visitors arrived in the town by train, charabanc and the occasional private car to breathe in the ozone and bathe in the briny. The harbour remained a focal point and a salt water bathing pond was constructed next to it. This view was taken in the 1950s, by which time the number of cars arriving in the town had risen dramatically. Realising that there was a lucrative trade to be had, the town council started charging for parking at the seafront in 1920.

NORTH BERWICK FROM HARBOUR ROCKS.

1739.

To entertain the growing number of visitors, a small stage was erected on the esplanade beside the swimming pool, and even on stormy days (such as the one shown here) large crowds would gather to watch a troupe of pierrots, or a travelling circus, or such acts as Erick's Entertainers, the Kentucky Operatic Minstrels, Lynn and Allan's Entertainers or the Joe Anderson Group. Despite Joe Anderson's vociferous opposition, work began in 1930 on a permanent, indoor music hall beside the site of the outdoor arena.

At the Swimming Pool, North Berwick

The pool first appeared in rudimentary form in 1905 when a group of locals belonging to the North Berwick Swimming Club engaged Messrs Belfrage and Carfrae to construct a simple bathing pond on the site of a rubbish dump on the Platcock Rocks. Simple wooden shacks were built as changing facilities and later a larger shed called The Ark was constructed: boys to the left; girls to the right! Despite some early problems with opposition to mixed bathing, the pool thrived and a swimming instructor was appointed in 1913. In 1919 a new electric pump was installed to draw in fresh sea water at the rate of two-and-a-half feet every five hours.

"THE FLIGHT OF THE SWALLOWS." BATHING POND, NORTH BERWICK. A.992.

Another popular attraction was the Swimming Gala with its races, tin-can retrieval exercises, synchronised swimming and diving displays featuring such experts as American Pete Desjaidin or, in the 1950s and sixties, the Scottish Commonwealth Games Champion, Peter Heatley. Or there might be a Canadian champion log-roller or a demonstration from Pond Masters McCracken, Lemmon or Kennedy. Crowds of up to 3,000 spectators were attracted to such events. Behind the three high-divers in this picture is the Harbour Pavilion which opened its doors as an entertainment centre in 1931. It was demolished in 1998 and the site used for the Scottish Seabird Centre.

15

An extensive renovation between 1927 and 1929 saw the pool deepened and new concrete changing cubicles built along three sides. In the thirties a long, metal chute replaced the older wooden one and a two-tier diving platform – towering some 25 feet above water level – was built from tubular steel. A radio gramophone supplied the music for the hardy swimmers, and illuminated evening shows and midnight swims were started. A filtration and gas heating system was installed in the early 1960s, making it the first outdoor heated pool in Scotland: the water sometimes reaching the hitherto unprecedented temperature of 70°. Sadly, the costs of maintaining such a facility for a short, thirteen-week season, led to the pool's closure in August 1995. To the right of this view, posted in 1957, is the coastguard station and, to its left, the island of Craigleith. In the early nineteenth century the town council found themselves in financial difficulties and opted to arrange a lottery with the first prize being Craigleith Island. This was voted illegal, however, and Sir Hew Dalrymple bought the island for £400.

Right: The *New Statistical Account* of 1839 relates that 'A boat with eight men for the suppression of smuggling is stationed at North Berwick'. This view by the famous North Berwick postcard illustrator, Reginald Phillimore, recaptures a smuggling scene at the foot of the cliffs on which Tantallon Castle is situated. Standing solidly across an unclimbable precipice, and built with walls up to fourteen feet thick, the castle gave rise to a phrase which summarised the impossible: 'Ding doon Tantallon? Mak a brig to the Bass'. Sadly, the Cromwellian army of General Monck did not know the saying, and their cannon destroyed the building in 1650. In the distance is the island also mentioned in the old expression: the Bass Rock.

Left: Traditionally, the Bass marks the spot where the North Sea meets the Firth of Forth. Legend also has it that St Baldred, the seventh century Christian missionary, lived here in a hermit's cell. By the fourteenth century the Lauder family had acquired the island from the church and built a fortress on it, and Lauder Castle hosted Prince James (later King James I) before he set sail for France. On the way, he was kidnapped by the English and spent nineteen years in captivity. On his release he had the traitor Sir Walter Stewart incarcerated in the Bass prison. Later, the island was taken by Cromwell and then Lord Lauderdale bought it on behalf of the government to be used as a prison. Several Covenanters were placed in its grim dungeons, including John Blackadder. In 1691 the Bass was seized by four Jacobites who declared the island the last piece of British soil to be held by the Stewarts. William of Orange ordered the demolition of the prison and in 1706 the Bass passed into the keeping of the Dalrymple family.

STUDYING BIRD LIFE ON BASS ROCK
M.L. 'ST BALDRED' SERIES.

An account of 1839 describes how young gannets were captured. 'These large, white birds, measuring six feet from tip to tip of the wings . . . are taken from the rock by the keeper who descends with a rope fastened around his waist, and held above by his assistant. He lays hold of the bird with a hook, draws it towards him and kills it with a stroke on the head; then with great force he throws it over the rock to the sea below where men in a boat pick it up.

The Lairds of the Bass let out the grazing to the innkeeper at Canty Bay, who kept about thirty sheep on the island. He also had the right to take solan geese: the famous gannets which still inhabit the crag to the number of some 50,000! Sometimes these birds, with their distinctive fishy flavour, were sold and eaten in his inn. In return he had to convey passengers out to the island – initially in a small sailing smack and later in steam boats such as the *Puffin* and the *Bonnie Doon*. In 1902 a lighthouse was constructed on the ruins of the old Bass prison, and a succession of three keepers tended the light for 86 years until it was automated using solar power in 1988.

ISLAND OF FIDRA AND LIGHTHOUSE.

10760 (JV)

The other lighthoused island off North Berwick is Fidra. The origins of the name are obscure but might derive from 'feather island' – on account of the proliferation of eider ducks which nest there. The large opening through the rock is called the White Lady after the shape it is said to resemble. The lighthouse was built in 1885 by descendants of Robert Louis Stevenson, who may himself have been inspired by Fidra (which he knew well from his childhood visits to North Berwick) to write his novel *Treasure Island*. A small harbour exists below the light and a narrow-gauge railway linked it with the house itself, enabling supplies to be brought up the 113 feet from sea level. In October 1970, following the connection of the lamp to the mains electricity supply, the last keepers left the island.

The picturesque location of North Berwick belies its threatening situation. Rocky outcrops, heavy seas and sudden squalls can all spell danger for the unwary seaman. In 1857 a Rocket Brigade was established: their apparatus being kept in the porch of the old kirk by the harbour. In 1860 the town was allocated its first lifeboat, the 30-foot, ten-oared *Caroline* which was kept in a newly constructed boathouse in Shore Street. Three other boats followed: the *Caroline II*; the *Freemason* and the *Fergus Ferguson*. Several notable rescues were carried out, mostly off the treacherous rocks at Seacliff or near Craigleith Island, and in the gale-tossed seas off the west of the harbour. The lifeboat house (seen in the right centre of this picture) was reconstructed and enlarged in 1901.

Right: The *Norman Clark* arrived on station in December 1902. The incident depicted on this card, hand painted by local postcard artist Reginald Phillimore, probably occurred on 27 February 1903 when the lifeboat was launched under the command of coxswain John Thorburn into a full south-westerly gale to go to the aid of a stricken fishing smack, the *Providence*. On its return, the lifeboat could not make harbour and had to be rescued by a passing steamer. Thorburn remained in charge of the *Norman Clark* until his death in 1914. His funeral was a grand affair – the coffin being carried on the shoulders of his crew into the cemetery in Kirk Ports where the Rev. J. R. Burt performed the ceremony. Two other lifeboats later served the town: the *John William Dudley* and the *Elizabeth Moore Garden*. For forty-one years no lifeboat was stationed in North Berwick until 1966 when a children's TV programme raised the money to buy *Blue Peter III*. The present ILB, *Blue Peter 7*, was commissioned in 1994.

the "NORMAN CLARK" to the Rescue: A ship in distress off NORTH BERWICK.

Left: The North Berwick coastguards were stationed in this little whitewashed building on the Auld Kirk Green, sometimes called Anchor Green. Outside it the local contingent would parade in bell-bottomed sailor suits with drawn cutlasses and telescopes. A sixty-one foot signal mast was erected and storm cones were hoisted when needed. The monument on the right records the brave actions of Kate Watson who was drowned trying to rescue a boy from the sea in 1889. Previously the site had been used for the town's first church and burial ground. In 1951 the remains of the Auld Kirk were excavated by Dr James Richardson. The church was dedicated to St Andrew in 1177 and must have been used by pilgrims on their way to Fife, as several pilgrims' badges were found on the site. The most famous historical connection, however, dates to 1590 when a Black Sabbath took place, reputedly attended by Satan himself and 200 witches.

As can be seen from this aerial view, the Auld Kirk Green at the harbour was reached by a narrow strip of land and was almost inaccessible at high tide. This gave the satanic gathering of 1590 a remote, isolated place in which to indulge their diabolical practises. It was also easy to find some of the prime ingredients for their sorcery: human bones. The old graveyard in which such notables as the Lauders of the Bass were buried was continually being exposed by high tides, and grisly remains were easily obtained. At her trial, the accused witch, Agnes Sampson, confessed to tying parts of a dead man and several joints of his body to a cat which was then drowned at sea in an attempt to conjure up a storm which would overwhelm the King of Scots on his return from Denmark. The attempt failed, but it was perhaps divine retribution which saw great storms sweep away the eastern part of the kirk and a large section of the graveyard in 1656. Recent excavations in the area, carried out during the construction of the National Seabird Centre, have uncovered many interesting burials which could possibly date back to the tenth century.

It was probably with some relief that the kirk at the harbour was abandoned. It had long been associated with witchcraft – and probably later inspired Robert Burns to write his famous poem of the supernatural, *Tam o' Shanter*. Some of the stone from the Auld Kirk was used (along with newly quarried Law stone) to build a new church, dedicated to St Andrew, on ecclesiastical land called Well Croft, some distance away from the Anchor Green. It eventually cost £200 and was dedicated in 1664. It was built to a post-Reformation pattern to accommodate 500 members of the congregation sitting lengthwise in box pews, facing a pulpit which was set in the centre. There were two garreted lofts for the major landed proprietors: the Dalrymples and the Grant Sutties.

While the new church was being built in Kirk Ports, the burgh parishioners met in the 'Great Tenement' of Sir Andrew Dick. It stood on a site to the left of this view of Quality Street (originally called Market Street or Trongate). In earlier times, weekly markets were held in this street beside the market cross. Goods would be weighed on the public tron or weighing machine. King Robert II recognised the town's importance as a commercial centre when he confirmed the right of the first Earl of Douglas to erect a tron, which remained in use until 1751. The name Quality Street probably derived from the fact that some of the principal residences of 'people of quality' were constructed on this road, leading down to the harbour. Here stood the principal inn and post house, and also, at the very end of the street, The Lodge, the town house of the Dalrymple family who are recorded as living here from 1697. This was sold to the town council in 1939 and the grounds made into a public park. The group of buildings was renovated for resale by the National Trust for Scotland in 1964.

The street's connection with 'quality' continued in October 1902 when King Edward VII visited the town and planted a tree in Quality Street. His hosts were his relations, Prince and Princess Edward of Saxe Weimar, who were staying at The Knoll, the property of Dr G. A. Berry. The house was thereafter known as King's Knoll! The Saxe Weimars planted a tree next to King Edward's tree, and the event is shown in this picture, with the royal dignitaries flanked by Provost James Macintyre, the town council and a contingent of the local Volunteer Rifle Corps. The volunteer corps was subsequently incorporated into the Territorial Army as part of local MP Richard Haldane's army reforms.

St. Baldreds Tower, North Berwick.

In its heyday as a watering hole and spa, great houses were built in North Berwick for the Tennant family (Glenconner), the De Zoetes (Ormesdene in Fidra Road), Esmonds (Marly Knowe), Balfours (Glasclune in Greenheads Road), Waldorf Astors (Shipka), Crees (Tusculum), and Asquiths (Hyndford). St Baldreds Tower, above, was built in Greenheads Road in 1885 for the Chambers family. In this picture the family appear to be lounging in the gardens, taking afternoon tea beside the croquet lawn. The building became a nursing home in 1934 and has recently been converted into flats.

FROM MARINE HOTEL NORTH BERWICK

W. NIEBECKER, MANAGER.

To cater for the growing influx of summer visitors, many large hotels were built during the second half of the nineteenth century. The Marine Hotel was constructed between 1875 and 1876 by J. and R. Whitecross at a cost of £25,000. It was a majestic establishment, measuring 160 by 60 feet and boasting 54 bedrooms, an outside balcony to sample the sea breezes, a well-stocked library, thermal and medicinal baths and servants' quarters in the attic. In 1880 a new wing to the west created an additional 27 guest suites. On 17 March 1882, disaster struck, however, and the hotel was totally destroyed by fire. Little time was lost in building a replacement and the architect, Mr Pilkington, designed the building seen in this 1886 picture. The new Marine was put under the management of Wilhelm Niebecker, a 38 year old German who arrived with his wife, two children and a 19 year old nanny. The staff of thirty under his charge waited hand and foot on the elegant guests who began to pour in. Proximity to the golf course was one of the main attractions of the Marine Hotel.

Right: The clubhouse for North Berwick Golf Club was built on the site of the old toll house – the little whitewashed cottage in the centre of this picture. To the right stands the gasometer of the town gasworks, built here in 1860-61. The works were not removed until 1905 when production was transferred to Williamston, at which point the gas container and 90-foot tower were bought and demolished by the manager of the Royal Hotel, Colin Campbell, to allow tennis courts and croquet greens to be laid out. Permission to build the clubhouse had to be sought from the Westgate Feuars or 'Coo Club' as it was colloquially called. For years the club had paid feu duty to this organisation, whose members owned property in the Westgate (at that time the area between the Law Road and Abbey Road) and who had won the right in 1800 to graze their animals on the West Links.

NORTH BERWICK FROM PT. GARRY

Left: The Baron Bailie of the Coo Club had several difficult situations to cope with. In 1821, several members removed more than their due quota of turfs from the links (either to roof their houses or cover their family graves) and fines had to be imposed. Other fines were levied for damage done to the links by carters driving cart loads of stones and sand from the beach, and farmers taking loads of seaweed across the links to be used as fertiliser. This early view may show seaweed being collected before being carried inland – perhaps up the street named after this practice: Ware Road. Behind the horses are two bathing huts – constructed to allow female bathers to undress in decency, and behind them is the links area traditionally used by fishermen for drying their nets. The beach in front was often covered with herring boats and R. L. Stevenson mentions playing among these craft in *The Lantern Bearers.*

29

Right: A golf club was established on the West Links under the auspices of the Golf Club of St Andrews in 1832. It comprised 'fifty noblemen and gentlemen from all parts of the country' who were admitted by ballot, one black ball excluding. The course was laid out on land which had once belonged to the Cistercian nunnery, with an additional area being purchased from Colonel Grant in 1922. In 1880 a single-storey clubhouse was built (visible on the extreme right of this view). Later, an upper storey was added. Also visible in this late nineteenth century photograph is the St Andrews Manse (high up, on the left) built amidst six acres of glebe lands in 1824-25. The other solitary, elevated building is Greenend in Bank Street, built around 1890.

First Tee, North Berwick.

Left: Amongst its last entries, the Coo Club minute book mentions the construction of a shelter shed for caddies and the extension of the starter's facilities on the first tee. Golf has been played in North Berwick for centuries, and a town council record of 1728 states that 'intimation be publicklie made that no person play at the gowff to prejud the growing of grass on the common green on Burgh Common'. This was at the east end of town – from East Road to the Millburn. The West Links course originally only had seven holes before being extended to the wall at the Redan Tee when nine holes were played. By the Edwardian era the course stretched to eighteen holes. The first recorded professional golfer and greenkeeper was David Strath, appointed in 1876, and other famous personalities of the links included Davie Grant, Harry Vardon, James Braid, Ben Sayers and Open champion Bob Ferguson.

In the first decades of the twentieth century thousands of golfers and holidaymakers poured into North Berwick during the summer months. Bus companies such as Scottish Motor Traction, Stark's and Fowler's laid on coaches and charabancs to cater for the influx of visitors. This splendid vehicle is a 1931 Bedford Sunsaloon, its canvas top duly rolled back in the sunshine. The photograph was taken on the links near Westerdunes House, and the vehicle is probably heading for the main bus stance in Church Road, alongside the Abbey Church.

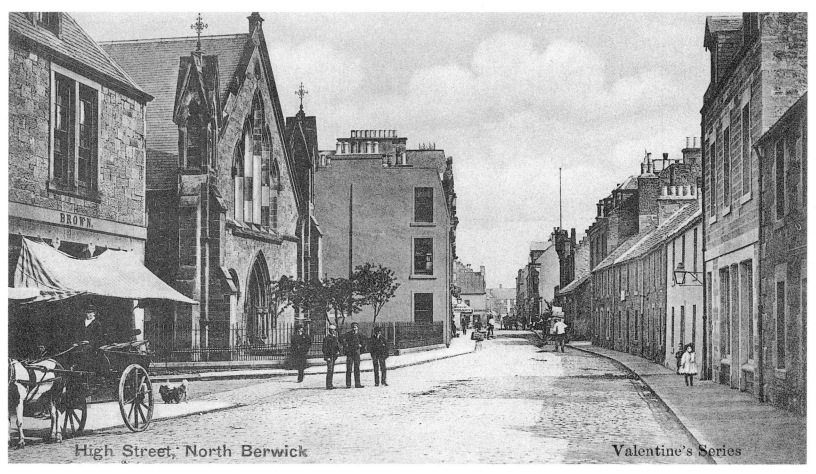

High Street, North Berwick   Valentine's Series

The Abbey Church, on the left beside Brown the Bakers, was built in 1868 to house the United Presbyterian congregation. The old properties on the right, facing the church, were demolished in 1904 and the Golfers Rest Public House built in their place. The flagpole in the centre right is on the facade of St Andrews Church, designed in 1882 by R. Rowand Anderson to replace the parish church in Kirk Ports. This picture predates the building of the church's 90-foot tower, erected in 1907. The low building in the centre, in front of which a street sweeper is hard at work, is the Foresters' Hall, built in 1887 for the Ancient Order of Foresters but latterly used as a dance hall, show room, roller skating venue and theatre. In 1938 Thomas Scott converted it into the 1,000-seater Playhouse Cinema. This was demolished in the mid-1980s and flats built in its place.

The High Street had been causeyed as early as 1688, and to cater for increased nineteenth century horse traffic new cobblestones were laid in 1862. Eventually, in the 1920s, the roadway was laid with asphalt tar. The building facing the camera on the left was a shop belonging to the family firm of Goodall's grocers. This area was the original 'shopping centre' of North Berwick, and in the early 1800s the town council let out three flesher's stalls to local butchers. Later, a bakehouse and a smiddy joined the complex. Andrew Goodall set up his business in the 1860s and the family firm continued under his son, John, until the shop was demolished in the early 1930s. New tenements and shops were built on the site, next to a branch of the Haddington Cooperative Society which had opened in 1925. The crowd of locals in this mid-Victorian view are standing at the foot of Kay's Wynd (now Law Brae) down which the Clarty Burn flowed before it was piped underground in 1800. It originally flowed into the sea at the spot where the Hope Institute (now Hope Rooms) was built in 1898.

Right: Beyond Goodall's Corner stood property belonging to Ben Sayers, whose workshops produced the world famous golf clubs. Further up was what local historian, J. S. Richardson, called, in 1907, a 'rabbit warren' of wynds and alleys. Narrow lanes which once existed here included Dick's Close, Grieve's Close, Sommerville Court and Begbie's Court. Only one, Cats Close, remains. Next to it, on the right of this 1900 view, were two interesting eighteenth century buildings which unfortunately were demolished in 1933 to build a new police station, replacing the earlier one in Victoria Road. Numbers 41-43 High Street, opposite these buildings, were built in 1870.

North Berwick.
High Street looking West.

QUALITY STREET, NORTH BERWICK.

Left: At the corner of the High Street and Quality Street stands the Town House, which dates back to the sixteenth century. It contained a meeting room for the town council, a customs house and a 'thieves' hole' for debtors and criminal offenders. The belfry was added in 1724 and the clock installed by local manufacturer, Andrew Smith, in 1810. In the foreground is the delivery cart of John Macintyre, chemist, lemonade manufacturer and provost of North Berwick from 1899 to 1919. Behind the cart is the property of James Whitecross which was demolished in 1938.

2566.

WAR MEMORIAL AND EAST ROAD, NORTH BERWICK.

The town's war memorial stands on the corner of Quality Street and East Road. It was carved by Alexander Carrick to a design by J. S. Richardson, Inspector of Ancient Monuments for Scotland, who lived in the town, and features the bronze regimental crests of the regiments of the 154 local soldiers who fell in the First World War. The pillar, topped by a unicorn, is in the form of a market cross. The building to its left was one of a group of town houses built for the Dalrymple family. To the right is 'Beulah', on the corner of School Road, named after the public school which was built there in 1876 and which now serves as the town museum. Provost Peter Brodie, chief magistrate at the turn of the twentieth century, lived in this area, and the new housing development replacing the eighteenth century buildings at the top of the road has been named Brodie Court in his honour. Previously, this area contained some fairly run-down buildings including the Toon Barn which held the burgesses' cows. The last herd was tended by Jennie McKellar whose byre and dairy stood halfway down Balfour Street.

A 3456

TENNIS COURTS & BASS ROCK, NORTH BERWICK.

McKellar's beasts grazed on the Town Common (still called the Coos' Green). This has been public land for generations, used for bleaching linen sheets, beating carpets, washing clothes and for recreational pursuits such as golf, sledging and putting. It may also have been the place where North Berwick's earliest settlers lived, as a neolithic shell midden was found on the Castle Hill – on the right of this card. Whether there ever was an early castle on this mound is still unclear, although an archaeological report in 1981 recommended that an excavation be undertaken to find out. Three tennis courts were built here in 1919 and a pavilion was added in the 1920s for the North Berwick Tennis Club. This was replaced in 1938, by which time the number of courts had risen to six.

The Coos' Green has played host to many local celebrations over the years, including the annual North Berwick Cycling Club Pageant, pipe band competitions and Easter parades. In the 1920s and thirties, a huge fund-raising fete and fancy dress contest was held every year on behalf of the Edinburgh Royal Infirmary. This picture of some of the fancy dress competitors dates from 1928.

EAST BAY, NORTH BERWICK.

There is no doubt that the recreational pursuit for which North Berwick became most famous was sea-bathing. As early as 1839, the author of the *New Statistical Account* was boasting that 'the geniality of summer is amply attested in the crowded influx of strangers for the enjoyment of sea bathing and perambulation'. An early guidebook explains why North Berwick air is so beneficial. 'This is in a great measure due to the diffusion in the atmosphere of chlorine and iodine vapours arising from the action of light and the sun's rays on the forms of marine growth such as kelp and tangle. This is known as ozone.' By the 1930s, hundreds were flocking to the beaches to swim, sail their boats in the yachting pond, take part in sand modelling competitions, sing with the Seaside Mission or eat an ice cream bought from a Luca's Rolls Royce ice-cream van. The low cottages in the centre were built for the local coastguards in 1868, while the three-storey tenements to their left replaced an iron foundry operated by Robert Bridges between 1830 and 1890.

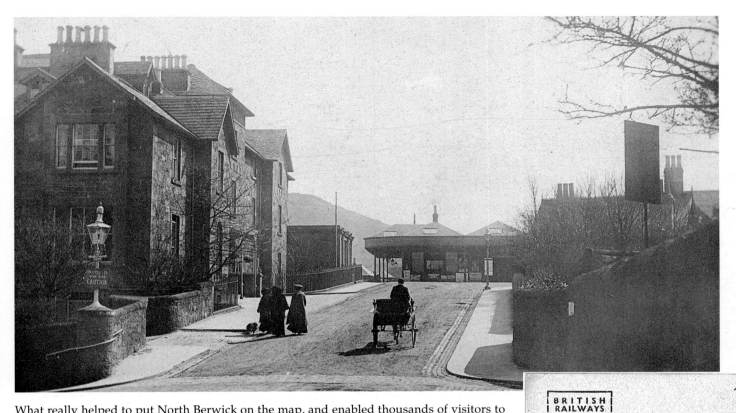

A luggage label to North Berwick issued by British Railways in the 1940s.

What really helped to put North Berwick on the map, and enabled thousands of visitors to flock into the town, was the railway. In June 1850 a branch line was completed linking North Berwick to the main Edinburgh-London line at Drem. The engineer, Alan Wilson, of the North British Railway Company, was duly made an honorary burgess of the royal burgh. The original stationmaster, William Scott, was immensely proud of his two-platform station, surrounded by an elegant, pillared roof with an interesting wooden scalloped edge (sadly all now demolished). Eight trains arrived daily, with first class passengers paying 5s 9d for a return from Edinburgh. This fare included free porterage of their luggage into the railway hotel, built in 1859 and, on account of a visit from the Prince of Wales, called the Royal Hotel (also now vanished, and replaced by flats). Less well-off passengers could travel third class for only 3s 9d return. Later, the line was taken over by London and North Eastern Railway Company and then, after nationalisation in 1947, by British Railways.

Old Abbey Road, North Berwick.

67985.

During the construction of the station goods yard in 1848, workmen uncovered some stone coffins. It was discovered that they had come from the old burial ground attached to North Berwick Abbey which stood to the south of Old Abbey Road. The abbey originated as a Cistercian nunnery dedicated to the Virgin Mary in the mid-twelfth century and became a very wealthy establishment possessing vast areas of land and the rights to all the mills of Kintreath on the Mill Burn. After the Reformation, the abbey and its lands were granted to Sir Alexander Home (the Gudeman of North Berwick) who built a dwelling house, The Newark, on the site. Although the abbey no longer provided hospitality for pilgrims, the area would appear to have kept its connection with the provision of caring facilities. This postcard was sent from Bemersyde and carries the message, 'This is a view of the rest house where Mrs Douglas has been in bed for six months with her stomach.' (Also visible is a sign for Gilbert's garage where my grandfather, James Cockburn, worked as a mechanic for many years.)

Right: Coaches and carriers travelling to Edinburgh from North Berwick passed through Dirleton, a tiny hamlet of some 92 families (*New Statistical Account*) living in stone cottages picturesquely situated around the village green. The origin of the name Dirleton is uncertain but may derive from Derili, King of the Picts, a friend of St Baldred. Until 1612 the village was ecclesiastically ruled from Gullane, but in that year the parish church was shifted to Dirleton. The population of 1,200 made their living from the rich farmland around the town, taking their produce to the weekly market at Haddington, seven miles to the south. Dirleton remains one of the loveliest villages in Scotland – the little rubble-stone, pantiled cottages in this 1904 card still standing next to the Open Arms Hotel. In the background are the farm buildings of Dirleton Mains, now entered through the sixteenth century arched gateway to Dirleton Castle.

Left: The Castle Hotel, standing strategically on the corner of the village green in Dirleton, owes its existence to the improving zeal of Mrs Hamilton Nisbet Ferguson. She was a descendant of Sir John Nisbet, an eminent Scottish lawyer who purchased the barony of Dirleton in 1663. Mrs Nisbet Ferguson encouraged the building of a new manse for the Dirleton clergy. She was instrumental in having the castle enclosed by a handsome wall, and she also persuaded a developer to contract the eminent architect, William Burn, to design a hotel for the village. Normally, Burn only designed elegant, country mansions such as Dundas Castle and Ratho Park for the aristocratic nobility of the Lothians, but persuaded by his influential patroness, he designed this simple country inn.

Gullane, the next village to Dirleton, is some five miles from North Berwick. The original spelling of Golyn, meaning 'little lake', referred not just to the village but to the whole parish, which incorporated Dirleton and Congalton. The original proprietors were the de Vaux family who donated several benefices upon the church in the village. As the religious establishment dedicated to St Andrew prospered, it became a valuable commodity and was owned at various times by the monks of Dryburgh, the Earls of Mar and Lord Cardross. By 1612 the village was in state of decay, sand-blown and largely deserted. It was decided to move the centre of the parish to Dirleton and a new church was built there (the old Gullane church was left to decay into its present, ruined state). However, the village subsequently prospered again. In this 1922 view Bisset's Hotel, famous with the golfing fraternity, is flourishing, while a delivery lorry from Barker & Hobson unloads Viking toffee and chocolate at the village shop, and a quaint vehicle stands at the door of Mr Aitken, clock maker.

The Smiddy, Gullane.

In addition to its famous golf courses, Gullane also acquired a reputation as a centre for training racehorses. It is recorded that as early as the thirteenth century the flat links were being used for exercising horses. By 1839 there were two famous equine training establishments, and over thirty horses were daily being exercised over the links and along the sand dunes which are a feature of the beaches at Gullane. Perhaps to cater for the large amount of horses in the town, a smiddy was situated in the Main Street, not far from the town common, the Goose Green. According to an early historian of the village, this blacksmith's forge was in the same family for many generations. The building, duly conserved, still stands in the centre of the village and operates as a florist.

Gullane's reputation as healthy resort, and its proximity to some seven golf courses, saw it becoming a popular place in which to live. A new row of two-storey houses with shops at street level were built in the late nineteenth century, and in neighbouring Hill Road several handsome villas were constructed including Purvesholm (1898), Sea House (1899), The Warren (1909), Whatton Lodge (1910), Coldstones (1912), Corner House (built by Robert Lorimer in 1912) and Belton (1924). To cater for the growing number of residents from south of the border, a new Episcopalian church (St Adrian's) was built in 1926.

Aberlady village. In 1795 three soldiers of Grant's Fencibles were accused of mutiny after they complained about the severity of their drill, and were sentenced to be shot on the links near the village of Aberlady. The whole regiment was lined up and 16 men were chosen as a firing squad. The rest of the regiment was disarmed and a troop of 32 men of the Scots Brigade were brought from Dunbar to stand by with loaded muskets in case of riot. Hundreds flocked out from Gullane and Aberlady to watch events unfold. It was then announced that one of the men would be reprieved. Lots were drawn and the lucky man 'capered and jumped about in an excess of joy'. The first soldier met the firing squad with bravado, dropping the signal handkerchief himself and falling dead on the first volley. The second began to panic and threw himself on the ground where he was shot at until his body was 'dreadfully mangled'. The bodies were carried on a cart into Aberlady where they were buried in the churchyard next to the fifteenth century kirk. Things look quieter in this 1900 view outside the Temperance Hotel!

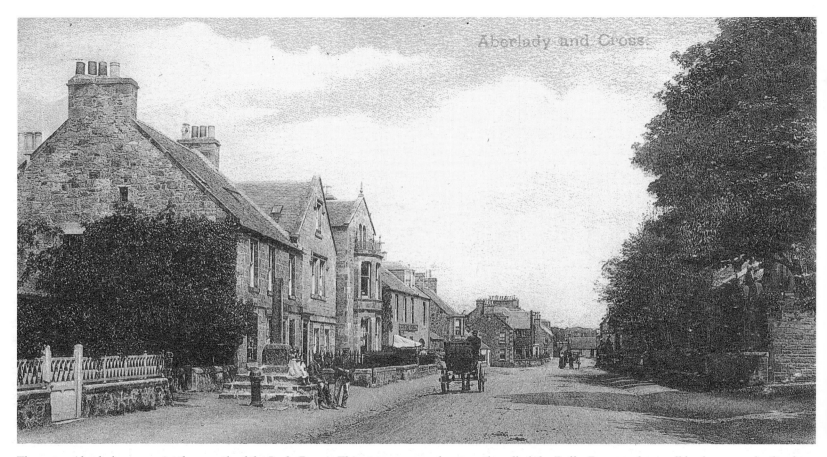

The name Aberlady means 'at the mouth of the Lady Burn'. This stream was subsequently called the Peffer Burn, and a small harbour was built where it flowed into the Forth. In 1624 King James VI confirmed Haddington's control over the port of Aberlady, and for many years the village continued to be the trading centre of Haddington, with the county town some four miles inland. By 1837 the village minister, the Rev. John Smith, was complaining that the trade was trifling. He was also unhappy at the fact that there were five inns in the parish, 'all licensed to sell ale and spirituous liquors: greater than can be looked upon with advantage'. He went on to say that the once thriving linen weaving trade in the village had vanished, leaving only a few minor trades and the profits from agriculture to sustain the economy. Later, some employment was supplied by the golf links at Kilspindie and at the Luffness course which was created by Tom Morris in the early 1870s. By then, however, the village market, which had taken place by the old Market Cross (the stump of which is visible on the left in this picture) had long since ceased to exist.

The Fishing Fleet, Aberlady.

60511. JV

The bay in which Aberlady harbour was situated had the unfortunate habit of silting up. By 1837 Rev. Smith was commenting that during the winter months the mudflats were frequented by large flocks of wild geese. Eventually, the harbour silted up completely and only a few (now converted) warehouses remain as evidence of Aberlady's once thriving sea port. Even so, a flourishing herring fishing industry continued, its success depending on the migratory habits of the fish. This postcard, sent in 1914, features no fewer than twenty boats pulled up on the foreshore in Aberlady Bay. Most of them would have remained there, as during the First World War the movement of fishing boats was severely restricted in the Forth. Many craft rotted away where they lay and their skeletal hulks are still visible at low tide.

"WHEN THE EVENING SUN IS LOW," NORTH BERWICK.

1592.

And here our tour of North Berwick and district comes to an end, as the evening sun dips over the Lamb Island. The name does not derive from the island's shape but from the Gaelic 'lamh' meaning a hill. The island rises to a height of 80 feet and is uninhabited – home only to seabirds such as the puffin and the cormorant. Seals also disport themselves on its rocky outcrops – called North Dog and South Dog. In the setting sun, the west bay off North Berwick – stretching out towards Dirleton and Gullane – is indeed a wonderful sight. As old North Berwick fishermen were wont to say, slightly misquoting Psalm 16, 'our lines have fallen in pleasant places'.